NEW YORK
JETS

BY JOSH ANDERSON

Stride

An Imprint of The Child's World®

childsworld.com

The Child's World
childsworld.com

Published by The Child's World®
800-599-READ • www.childsworld.com

ISBN Information
9781503857735 (Reinforced Library Binding)
9781503860612 (Portable Document Format)
9781503861978 (Online Multi-user eBook)
9781503863330 (Electronic Publication)

LCCN 2021952676

Printed in the United States of America

TABLE OF CONTENTS

GO JETS!

The New York Jets compete in the National Football **League's** (NFL's) American Football Conference (AFC). They play in the AFC East **division**, along with the Buffalo Bills, Miami Dolphins, and New England Patriots. The Jets play each of their divisional rivals twice per season. In 2021, the team had the chance to select second in the NFL Draft and chose Zach Wilson, an exciting young quarterback. Let's learn more about the Jets!

AFC EAST DIVISION

Buffalo Bills

Miami Dolphins

New England Patriots

New York Jets

WIDE RECEIVER COREY DAVIS (LEFT) JOINED THE JETS FOR THE 2021 SEASON.

5

BECOMING THE JETS

Originally called the New York Titans, the team began play in 1960. They were part of the American Football League (AFL). When new owners purchased the team in 1963, they changed the team's name to the Jets. In 1965, the team signed University of Alabama quarterback Joe Namath. Namath would become the most famous player in team history. He led the Jets to victory in their only **Super Bowl** appearance after the 1968 season.

QUARTERBACK JOE NAMATH AND HEAD COACH WEEB EWBANK TEAMED UP TO LEAD THE JETS IN THEIR SEASON OF GLORY.

BY THE NUMBERS

The Jets have won **ONE** Super Bowl.

FOUR trips to the AFC Championship Game for the jets

419 points scored by the Jets in 1968—a team record!

12 wins for the team in 1998

THE JETS PLAYED IN THE AFC CHAMPIONSHIP GAME IN 2009 AND 2010.

METLIFE IS ONE OF TWO STADIUMS SHARED BY TWO DIFFERENT NFL TEAMS.

METLIFE STADIUM

Since 1984, the New York Jets have played their home games in New Jersey. Their old home, Giants **Stadium**, and their current home, MetLife Stadium, are located in East Rutherford, New Jersey. East Rutherford is about 15 miles (24 km) away from New York City. The Jets share MetLife Stadium with the New York Giants, another NFL team. MetLife Stadium opened in 2010. It can hold more than 82,000 Jets fans on game days.

We're Famous!

The Jets logo got plenty of prime time airtime in the late 1980s and early 1990s. The main character on the hit ABC television show *The Wonder Years* was a huge fan. Actor Fred Savage played Kevin Arnold, who wore his New York Jets jacket in many episodes of the series. The show was set in the late 1960s, so the character got to live through a great era of Jets football.

UNIFORM

GREEN

WHITE

Truly Weird

In 1980, an NBC sports producer decided to try something different for the television broadcast of a game between the Jets and the Miami Dolphins. No announcers described the action on the field. The only sounds viewers heard were those coming straight from the stadium itself. The experiment was considered a failure and hasn't been tried since. The Jets won the game 24–17.

Alternate Jersey

Sometimes teams wear an alternate jersey that is different from their home and away jerseys. It might be a bright color or have a unique theme. The Jets wore New York Titans "throwback" uniforms for a game in 2011 against the Jacksonville Jaguars. The Jets won 32–3.

FANS IN NEW YORK HAVE BEEN CHEERING ON THE JETS FOR MORE THAN 60 YEARS.

Going to a game at MetLife Stadium can be a ton of fun. While many fans take public transportation to the game, those who drive often choose to tailgate. Tailgating fans make or serve food out of the back of their cars. It's a fun way for fans to connect before the game even starts. Fans celebrate good plays by shouting "J-E-T-S, Jets, Jets, Jets." While the Jets are one of the few teams without an official mascot, the Jets Flight Crew is a cheerleading squad that entertains the crowd at every home game.

JETS FLIGHT CREW

HEROES OF HISTORY

Mark Gastineau
Defensive End | 1979–1988

Gastineau led the NFL in sacks in 1983 and 1984, combining for 41 in those two seasons. His 107.5 career **sacks** rank first all-time for the Jets. Gastineau was chosen for the **Pro Bowl** five times during his career.

Don Maynard
Wide Receiver | 1960–1972

Maynard is the Jets' all-time leading receiver with 11,732 yards. His 88 receiving **touchdowns** rank 14th in NFL history. Maynard was a key player on the Jets team that won Super Bowl 3. He was chosen for four Pro Bowls. Maynard is a member of the Pro Football **Hall of Fame**.

Joe Namath
Quarterback | 1965–1976

Namath is the most iconic player in Jets history. A hero to many New Yorkers, Namath led the Jets to victory in Super Bowl 3. He was chosen for five Pro Bowls and is a member of the Pro Football Hall of Fame.

Darrelle Revis
Cornerback | 2007–2012, 2015–2016

Revis was one of the best defensive backs of his generation. The seven-time Pro Bowler even had a phrase named after him. When Revis lined up against a wide receiver, the receiver was said to be on "Revis Island." This meant the receiver had no way to get the football.

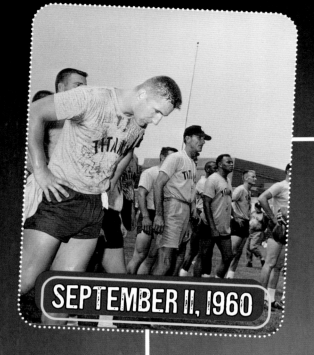

SEPTEMBER 11, 1960

The New York Titans defeat the Buffalo Bills 27–3 in the first game in franchise history.

The Jets defeat the Jacksonville Jaguars 34–24 and earn a trip to the AFC Championship Game.

JANUARY 10, 1999

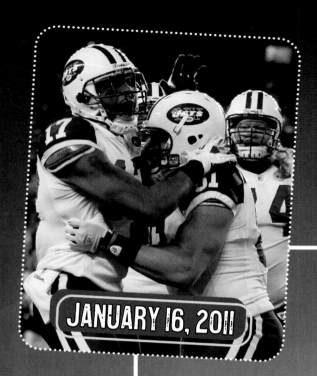

JANUARY 16, 2011

In a **playoff** matchup with their divisional rival, the Jets defeat the New England Patriots to reach the AFC Championship Game.

With the second overall selection in the NFL Draft, the team selects Zach Wilson, a quarterback from Brigham Young University.

WILSON

1

APRIL 29, 2021

MODERN-DAY MARVELS

Michael Carter
Running Back | Debut: 2021

The Jets picked Carter in the fourth round of the 2021 NFL Draft after his successful college career at the University of North Carolina. Carter immediately worked his way into the Jets lineup. Carter totaled 964 yards from scrimmage and four total touchdowns as a rookie.

Corey Davis
Wide Receiver | Debut: 2021

Davis spent his first four pro seasons with the Tennessee Titans. He finished 2020 with 984 yards and five touchdowns. Davis signed with the Jets as a free agent in 2021. He's been at his best in the playoffs, with three touchdown catches in six career games.

C. J. Mosley
Linebacker | Debut: 2019

Mosley spent his first five seasons with the Baltimore Ravens. He signed with the Jets as a free agent in 2019. He's finished in the top ten in combined tackles two times. Mosley has earned four trips to the Pro Bowl.

Zach Wilson
Quarterback | Debut: 2021

The Jets chose Wilson second in the 2021 NFL Draft. He won the quarterback job in training camp and started the first game of his **rookie** year. Wilson's first victory with the Jets was a 27–24 **overtime** win over the Tennessee Titans.

CURTIS MARTIN WAS INDUCTED INTO THE PRO FOOTBALL HALL OF FAME IN 2012.

THE GOAT

GREATEST OF ALL TIME

CURTIS MARTIN

Martin rushed for more than 1,000 yards in ten-straight seasons from 1995 to 2004. The Jets' all-time leader in rushing yards, he finished his time in New York with 10,302 rushing yards. Martin's career total of 14,101 rushing yards ranks sixth in NFL history. His 90 rushing touchdowns are tied for 13th all-time. Martin was chosen for five Pro Bowls in his career. He is a member of the Pro Football Hall of Fame.

#1

FAN FAVORITE

Wayne Chrebet—Wide Receiver
1995–2005

After his great college career at Hofstra University, no NFL team chose Chrebet in the NFL Draft. It is hard for an undrafted player to earn a place on a team's roster, so when he made the Jets' team in training camp in 1995, Chrebet became an immediate fan favorite. Chrebet finished his career as the third-leading receiver in franchise history with 7,365 yards.

THE BIG GAME

The Jets had never reached the postseason before the 1968 season. After defeating the Oakland Raiders in the AFL Championship Game, the Jets advanced to the Super Bowl. Their opponent would be the Baltimore Colts, the NFL champions. Led by quarterback Johnny Unitas, the Colts were expected to win by more than two touchdowns. Before the game, Jets All-Pro quarterback Joe Namath publicly promised New York fans a win. The Jets scored their only touchdown in the second quarter but added three more field goals later. When the game was over, the Jets came out victorious 16–7.

THE AFL-NFL CHAMPIONSHIP GAME BETWEEN THE JETS AND THE COLTS WAS ALSO KNOWN AS THE THIRD WORLD CHAMPIONSHIP GAME.

WEEB EWBANK LED THE TEAM TO 71 VICTORIES BETWEEN 1963 AND 1973.

AMAZING FEATS

 **31** Touchdown Passes

In 2015 by **QUARTERBACK** Ryan Fitzpatrick

 **14** Rushing Touchdowns

In 2009 by **RUNNING BACK** Thomas Jones

 **1,502** Receiving Yards

In 2015 by **WIDE RECEIVER** Brandon Marshall

 **14** Receiving Touchdowns

In 1960 by **WIDE RECEIVER** Art Powell

ALL-TIME BEST

PASSING YARDS

Joe Namath
27,057

Ken O'Brien
24,386

Richard Todd
18,241

RUSHING YARDS

Curtis Martin
10,302

Freeman McNeil
8,074

Emerson Boozer
5,135

RECEIVING YARDS

Don Maynard
11,732

Wesley Walker
8,306

Wayne Chrebet
7,365

SACKS*

Mark Gastineau
107.5

Joe Klecko
78

Shaun Ellis
72.5

SCORING

Pat Leahy
1,470

Nick Folk
729

Jim Turner
697

INTERCEPTIONS

Bill Baird
34

Dainard Paulson
29

Darrelle Revis
25

*unofficial before 1982

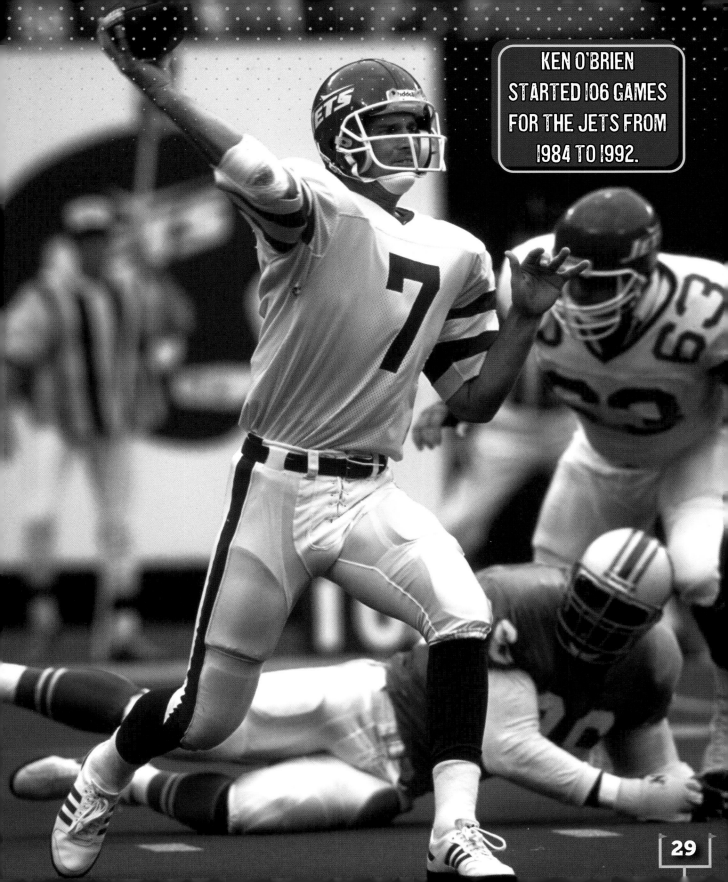

KEN O'BRIEN STARTED 106 GAMES FOR THE JETS FROM 1984 TO 1992.

GLOSSARY

division (dih-VIZSH-un): a group of teams within the NFL who play each other more frequently and compete for the best record

Hall of Fame (HALL of FAYM): a museum in Canton, Ohio, that honors the best players in NFL history

league (LEEG): an organization of sports teams that compete against each other

overtime (OH-vuhr-tym): extra time that is played when teams are tied at the end of four quarters

playoffs (PLAY-ahfs): a series of games after the regular season that decides which two teams play in the Super Bowl

Pro Bowl (PRO BOWL): the NFL's All-Star game where the best players in the league compete

rookie (RUH-kee): a player playing in his first season

sack (SAK): when a quarterback is tackled behind the line of scrimmage before he can throw the ball

stadium (STAY-dee-uhm): a building with a field and seats for fans where teams play

Super Bowl (SOO-puhr BOWL): the championship game of the NFL, played between the winners of the AFC and the NFC

touchdown (TUTCH-down): a play in which the ball is brought into the other team's end zone, resulting in six points

IN THE LIBRARY

Bulgar, Beth and Mark Bechtel. *My First Book of Football.*
New York, NY: Time Inc. Books, 2015.

Jacobs, Greg. *The Everything Kids' Football Book, 7th Edition*.
Avon, MA: Adams Media, 2021.

Sports Illustrated Kids. *The Greatest Football Teams of All Time*.
New York, NY: Time Inc. Books, 2018.

Wyner, Zach. *New York Jets*. New York, NY: AV2, 2020.

ON THE WEB

Visit our website for links about the New York Jets:
childsworld.com/links

Note to parents, teachers, and librarians: We routinely verify our web links to make sure they are safe and active sites. Encourage your readers to check them out!

ABOUT THE AUTHOR

Josh Anderson has published over 50 books for children and young adults. His two boys are the greatest joys in his life. Hobbies include coaching his sons in youth basketball, no-holds-barred games of Apples to Apples, and taking long family walks. His favorite NFL team is a secret he'll never share!

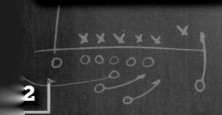